MW01516250

Beer on th
The Craft Breweries of Alaska

Volume One: Kenai Peninsula and Kodiak Island Breweries

By Bill Howell
Photos by Elaine Howell

Bill Howell

Foreword by Jim "Dr. Fermento" Roberts

It's about time someone wrote a book about Alaska's great beer. It's long overdue. I started writing about beer as a columnist for the Anchorage Press in 1997 and since then, I've seen Alaska's craft beer industry literally explode across this vast state. When I started writing, I could count Alaska's operating breweries with the fingers on one hand. Today, Alaska boasts over 20 noteworthy brewing operations that keep locals well-watered and continue to bait the beer-curious visitors to the state. When it comes to beer in Alaska, there's a lot to say, and I can't think of anyone better to take on such a project than Bill Howell.

Maybe Bill's a bit newer to the beer scene than I am, but in my opinion, he's infinitely more qualified to produce this beautiful guide and tribute to beer in the vast confines of the 49th state. I first met Bill when he invited me to the Kenai Peninsula to be a guest speaker at his course, The Art and History of Beer, at the Kenai Peninsula College. Back then, there were just a few breweries; far less than in the foamier Anchorage Bowl, but Bill was teaching the only accredited beer course in Alaska. I was honored to travel to the Peninsula and address his students, and do so joyfully year after year when the class is offered.

About the Authors

One of the first questions I always ask about any guidebook is this: "What qualifies the author to give me advice on this particular subject or place?" So I think it's only fair that I tell you a little bit about myself.

I've been a craft beer lover and homebrewer since 1989. From 1984 to 2004, I was an officer in the United States Navy, which allowed me to travel extensively and sample beers all over the world. From 1998 to 2001, I was fortunate enough to be stationed in London, and during those three years I travelled throughout Britain, as well as to Belgium, Germany, and the Czech Republic to sample the best beers each had to offer.

I retired from the Navy in 2004 and moved to Sterling on Alaska's Kenai Peninsula, taking a job at Kenai Peninsula College, which is part of the University of Alaska. As craft breweries and brewpubs began opening in the area, I convinced my college administration that it was time to offer a course on beer, and in the spring of 2007, I taught **The Art & History of Brewing** for the first time. It was a rousing success and I have taught it again four times since.

Given the popularity of my course, starting a blog seemed the next logical step. My purpose in writing **Drinking on the Last Frontier** was mainly to keep my students, current and former, apprised of local beer developments. Much to my surprise, my blog developed quite a following, both within and outside of Alaska. Its popularity was such that I was offered a monthly beer column in one of our local papers, **The Redoubt Reporter**, in November 2009.

2/27/2010 at the Wynkoop Brewing Company in Denver

As I was riding the wave of this success, my wife convinced me to enter the **Wynkoop Brewing Company**'s Beerdrinker of the Year contest in December 2009. I didn't think I had much of a chance, but I was selected as one of the three finalists, and in the head-to-head competition in Denver on February 27, 2010, I actually won, much to my amazement. Deciding to accept this as a sign, my wife and I attended the Great American Beer Festival that year, something I hadn't done since 1990.

Since then, I have continued my efforts to educate folks about craft beer and to promote Alaska's craft breweries, both within and outside the 49th state. In 2012, I was hired by the *Northwest Brewing News* as their correspondent for Alaska, and I also began working on this book project.

You will certainly notice the many excellent photographs which illustrate this book. These are the work of my beautiful and talented wife, Elaine Howell, who graciously agreed to take part in this project by supplying those photographs.

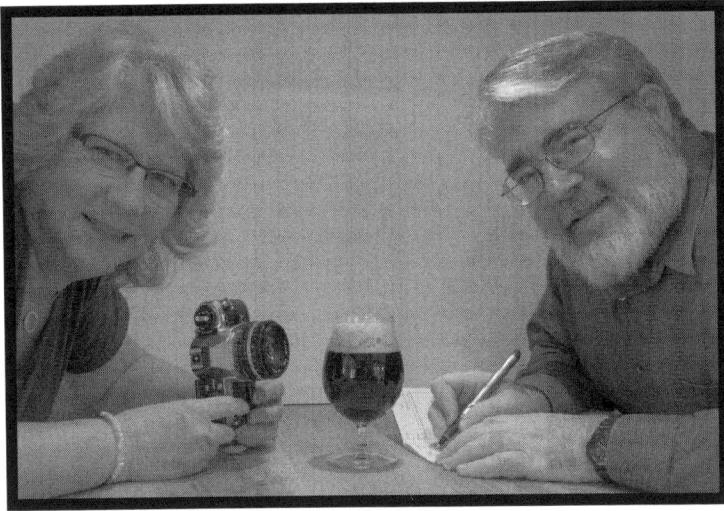

The authors, Elaine and Bill Howell

This book is the first in a series of three volumes which will describe the state of play of craft brewing in Alaska. As with any such guidebook, you may find that things have changed at a particular brewery since the time of writing; if so, please accept my apologies in advance. I intend to do my best to update the electronic version of this work on a regular basis, but the craft brewing scene in this state is a fast-moving target.

In spite of any such shortcomings, I hope you will find this work enlightening, entertaining, and useful. It represents a small gift back on my part to all the brewers who work hard every day to give us such exceptional beers to enjoy and to the citizens of the magnificent state of Alaska, which is now my home.

Introduction

As anyone who has ever been here can tell you, Alaska is a special place. Sometimes it's special in a good way, sometimes it's special in a bad way, but it's never ordinary. Here in The Great Land, we live a lot closer to the edge than most people do Outside (what Alaskans call the rest of the world). Those folks can tell themselves that Nature has been tamed by Man; we Alaskans know better.

Looking out the authors' living room window on 6/20/2011

It takes a certain kind of person to choose to live in a place as remote and rugged as Alaska. Some people are born to it, but choose to leave as soon as they can. Often they return after a year or two, finding nowhere else in the world holds the allure of the Far North. Others come up for a visit or a vacation or a job and never leave. Be Warned: If Alaska grabs hold of you, no other place in the whole wide world will ever seem like home again.

Tern Lake

Seward is a historic Alaskan town, founded in 1903. It serves as the southern terminus of both the Seward Highway and the Alaska Railroad, and is an important stop on the Alaska Marine Highway System, with cross-gulf ferries linking it to the capital Juneau in South-East Alaska. It is also a frequent cruise ship destination during the summer season. Located on the western side of Resurrection Bay, Seward has two primary commercial areas: the historic downtown surrounding Mile 0 of the Seward Highway, and the Seward Boat Harbor, adjacent to the cruise ship docks. A block north of the Alaska Sea-Life Center in downtown Seward you will find a brewpub, the **Seward Brewing Company**.

Resurrection Bay from downtown Seward

If instead of proceeding south to Seward, you turn on to the Sterling Highway at Tern Lake and follow it for another 160 miles or so, through the communities of Cooper Landing and Soldotna, you will eventually reach the town of Homer, the proverbial end of the road. For about half that distance you will be following the Kenai River, one of the greatest fishing locations in the world.

The twin cities of Soldotna & Kenai are located about half-way between Tern Lake and Homer, at about Mile 100 of the Sterling Highway. These two communities have very different origins, with Kenai dating to the Russian settlement of Alaska in the late 1700s, while Soldotna was established in 1947, the last town in the United States to be created on the basis of homesteading. Today, the boundary between the two cities is hard to discern, as they have more or less grown into each other over the last half century. Soldotna is home to both the **Kenai River Brewing Company** and the **St. Elias Brewing Company** brewpub, while **Kassik's Brewery** is located north of the city of Kenai, along the highway leading to the community of Nikiski.

Both Kenai and Soldotna have a mixed economy, combining oil and gas production in Cook Inlet with fishing the salmon runs of the Kenai River and surrounding streams, both commercially and via guided trips for sportsmen from around the world. The world famous Kenai king salmon is the fisherman's dream (the world record from the Kenai was 97 lbs.!), but the river also supports abundant runs of Sockeye (red) and Coho (silver) salmon, not to mention the lowly humpbacks (pinks).

After you cross the Kenai River one final time in Soldotna, you will find yourself driving along the eastern shore of the Cook Inlet, through small communities with names like Kasilof, Clam Gulch, Ninilchik, and Anchor Point, while gazing west across the inlet at the majestic volcanoes on the Alaska Peninsula. At last you will reach Homer, often called the Halibut Capital of the World, thanks to the abundance of that huge flat fish in the waters surrounding the town.

Homer was founded in 1896, originally as a port for coal mining, but by the middle of the century its focus had shifted to commercial fishing. In the late 1960s and early 70s, Homer was discovered by the artistic community. Today it is much less of a fishing port (though plenty of fishing does still go on, both commercial and by tourists) and much more of an arts colony, a "Cosmic Hamlet by the Sea," as some call it. You will find numerous art galleries and stores selling local crafts, both in the main business district along Pioneer Avenue and in the tourist area along the Homer Spit. Homer is also the jumping-off point for numerous tours and excursions, including trips to the world famous bear-viewing in Katmai National Park. **The Homer Brewing Company**, the first craft brewery on the Peninsula, is located just off the road leading down to the Homer Spit.

Aerial view of the Homer Spit

Kodiak Island

Approximately 130 miles southwest of Homer is Kodiak Island, the second largest island in the United States (after the Big Island of Hawaii). You can travel there either by a 70-minute flight from Anchorage or a nine-hour ferry ride from Homer. Kodiak is also home to the largest US Coast Guard base in the world, from which brave men and women fly across the stormy waters surrounding Alaska to rescue mariners in distress.

The seas around Kodiak are famous both for their storms and for their abundant seafood. The majority of the inhabitants of The Rock (as the island is affectionately known by those living there) make their living from some aspect of commercial fishing. The island is also famous for the Kodiak Bear, the largest of the subspecies of brown bears, with mature males weighing up to 1500 lbs., and there is a substantial tourist industry devoted to both sport fishing for salmon and bear viewing.

The town of Kodiak from Pillar Mountain

The town of Kodiak, founded by Russian traders in 1792, is the largest of seven communities on the island, and is its main commercial hub. It is also the location of the **Kodiak Island Brewing Company**.

Maps

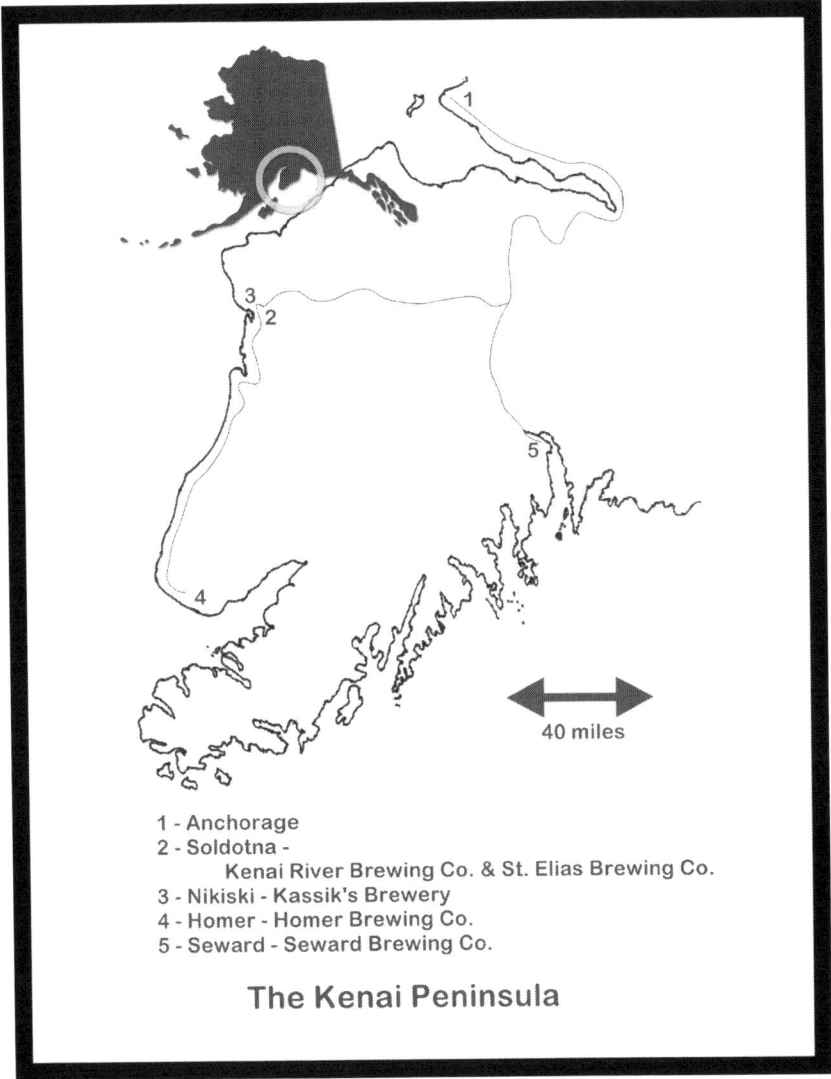

1 - Anchorage
2 - Soldotna -
 Kenai River Brewing Co. & St. Elias Brewing Co.
3 - Nikiski - Kassik's Brewery
4 - Homer - Homer Brewing Co.
5 - Seward - Seward Brewing Co.

The Kenai Peninsula

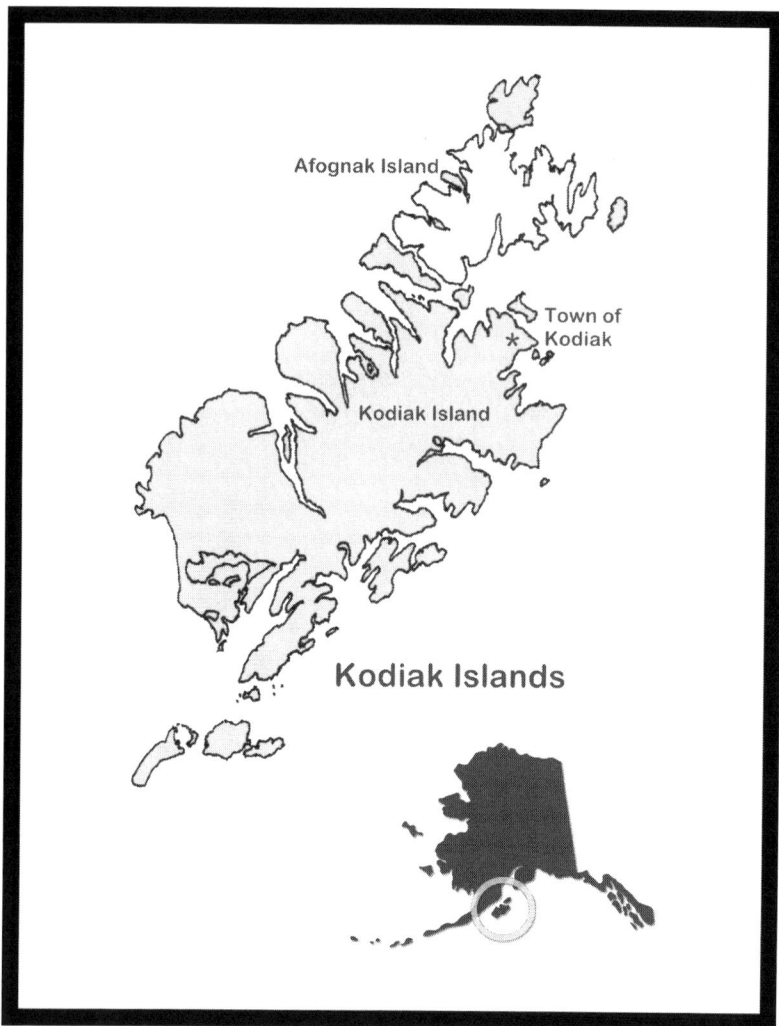

Afognak Island

Town of
Kodiak

Kodiak Island

Kodiak Islands

Kenai River Brewing Company

Location:

241 N. Aspen Dr.

Soldotna, AK 99669

Phone: 907-262-BEER (2337)

Email: beer@kenairiverbrewing.com

Website: www.kenairiverbrewing.com

Hours of Operation:

12 to 7 PM, Monday thru Saturdays. Closed on Sundays.

Driving Directions: From the Sterling Highway in Soldotna, turn on to the Kenai Spur Highway, heading toward the city of Kenai. At the second stoplight, turn left on to East Marydale Drive, then take the first left on to North Aspen Drive. The brewery will be a half block down on the right.

Overview

The brainchild of local schoolteacher and homebrewer Doug Hogue, Kenai River Brewing Company opened its doors in 2006. Working with his partner Wendell Dutcher, Hogue purchased a used 10-barrel brewhouse, installed it and several open fermenters in a former auto repair shop and brought his vision of a craft brewery in Soldotna to life.

Doug Hogue, Brewer & Owner

As is typical for the first craft brewery in a given area, much of the initial challenge Kenai River faced was to develop the local palate for craft beer. In a clever marketing move, for the first few years of the brewery's existence, each beer took its name from a particular fishing spot along the Kenai River. This helped create an immediate affinity for the brews among locals, as they immediately grasped the significance of each name.

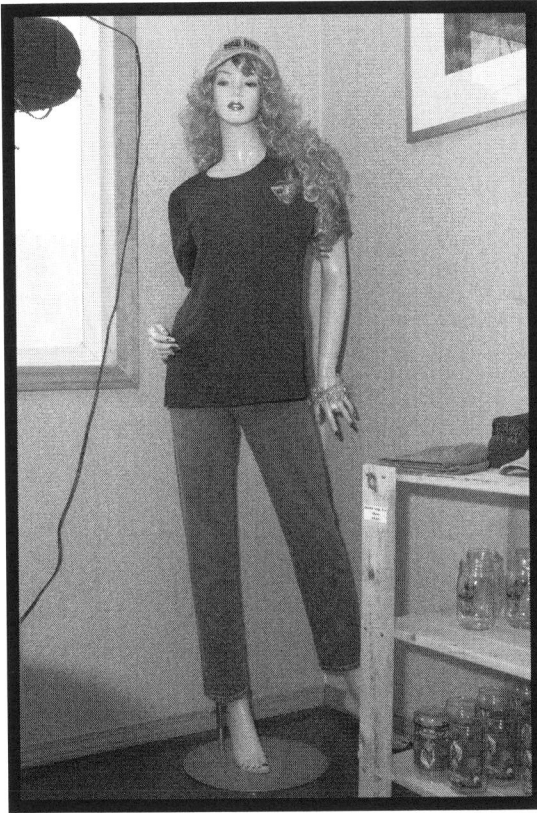

Inebriata, Kenai River Brewing's goddess

However, as soon as it was well established among the local beer culture, Kenai River began working to expand the envelope, initially by offering a series of *Single Hop IPAs*. This concept has become fairly familiar today, but was much less common in 2007 when Kenai River began brewing them. The basic concept is simple: brew a beer identical in every way possible to their standard *Sunken Isle IPA*, except that only a single variety of hop is used for bittering, flavor, and aroma. Six different Single Hop IPAs were offered in 2007 (Amarillo, Summit, Simcoe, Columbus, Centennial, & Cascade), each serving to showcase the characteristics of a single hop. The entire concept has proven quite popular with local craft beer lovers and Single Hop IPAs continue to be offered on an intermittent basis at the brewery to the present day.

Brewery Characteristics

The brewhouse at Kenai River is a steam-fired, 10-barrel system. Fermentation during the brewery's first years was exclusively open, and that is still the norm for most of the beers produced. However, with the start of canning operation in March, 2011, a 20-barrel conical closed fermenter was installed to increase production capability. Later, a second 20-barrel conical was installed when Doug and his team began canning a second beer style.

Brew kettle & mash tun

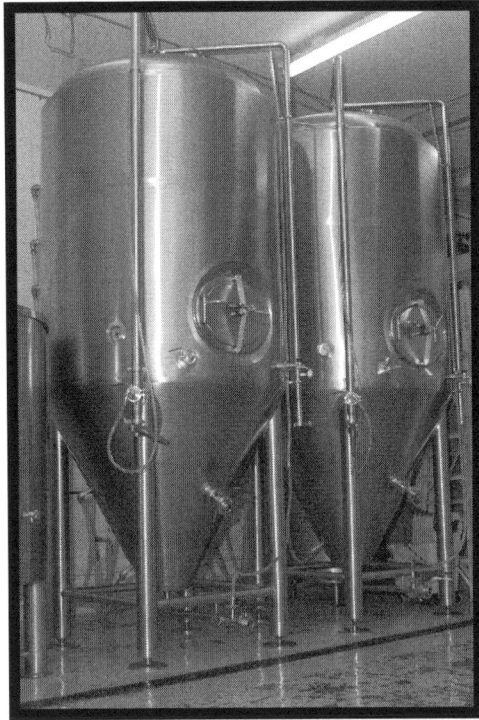

Open & conical fermenters

When Kenai River Brewing began offering its beer in cans, they were one of the first breweries in Alaska to do so. Hogue has stated that it had always been his intention to move into cans rather than bottles as soon as the brewery could support packaging. A can presents many obvious advantages for the beer drinker in Alaska. It's lighter (important when you must pack out everything you pack into the wilderness), unbreakable (nothing ruins a fishing trip on the Kenai faster than a boat full of broken beer bottle glass), and easily recyclable. Reception of their flagship *Skilak Scottish Ale* in the new package was extremely positive, resulting in a second beer, *Sunken Isle IPA*, being offered in cans in October of 2011.

Hand canning machine from Cask Brewing Systems

Besides cans, beers are available at the brewery by the 64 or 32-oz growler to take away, or by the pint for consumption in their Taproom. Some beers are also available in 2.25-gallon returnable plastic pigs and individual kegs may also be purchased. The Kenai River Taproom does not serve food, but patrons are welcome to bring in food from surrounding restaurants or even to have pizzas delivered there.

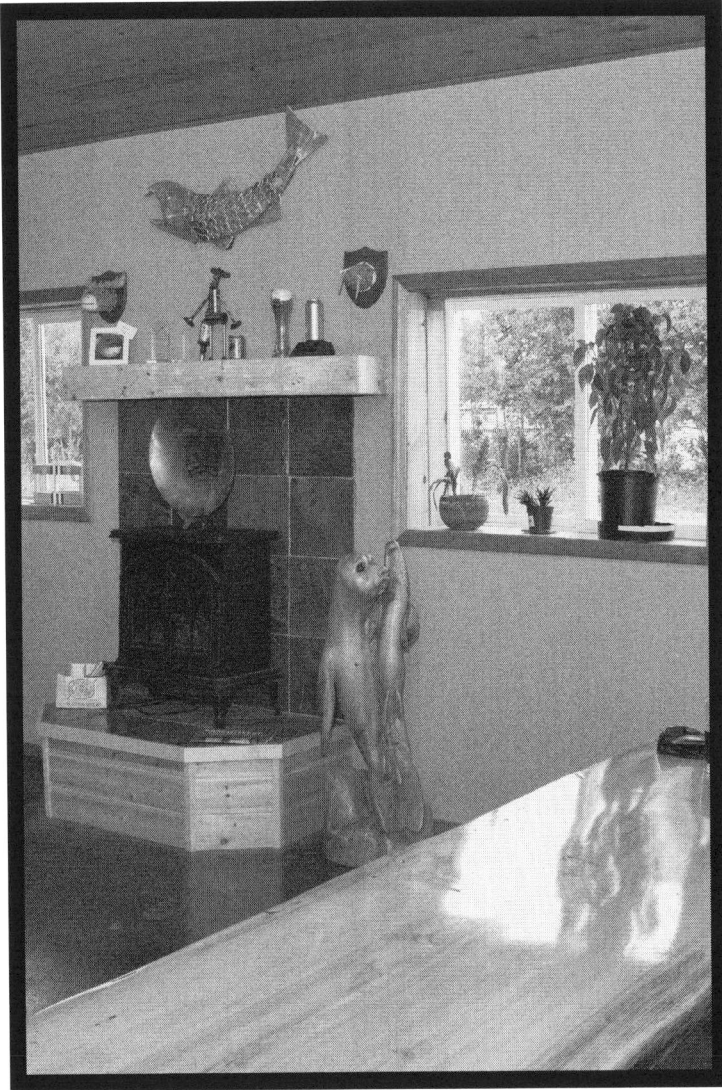

Kenai River Brewing's Tap Room

The Brewer Speaks

Brewer/Owner Doug Hogue in his own words:

How did you become a commercial brewer?

"I was an avid homebrewer for about 10 years before pursuing a commercial career in brewing. After moving to Soldotna, Alaska, I became friends with one of my current business partners, Wendell, who was also a homebrewer. One evening, after consuming a few of our creations, we decided to check into opening a local brewery in town. We built our business plan over the following year, found a nice little Specific Mechanical 10hl system, and the rest is history......."

What do you see as the biggest challenges facing a craft brewer in Alaska?

"Shipping costs!!!"

What characteristics do you think define Alaska craft beer, as opposed to craft beer brewed elsewhere?

"Brewers in Alaska tend to brew outside the style more often than not. Once the summer season is over, we typically brew beer more for ourselves and our local customers. For us, this often remains fun for our summer visitors as we try to save a half barrel of each of these brews and periodically tap them throughout the summer."

Where do you think Alaska craft brewing in general and your brewery/brewpub in particular will be in eight to ten years?

"Alaskan craft brewing will continue to grow throughout the state. Alaskans love to support local business and breweries certainly benefit from this. Folks in the Lower-48 are very intrigued with products made in Alaska, so this market certainly has plenty of opportunity also. We plan to continue to grow organically and will pursue markets as our growth allows."

The Beers

Regularly On-Tap

Skilak Scottish Ale: The first beer offered by Kenai River and still one of their top sellers. It pours dark amber with a light beige head. Its aroma is smooth malt along with a touch of smoke. On the palate there's deep, roasted malt flavor, finishing with a long, slightly sweet malt aftertaste. 5.3% ABV, 36 IBUs. Draft or cans.

Sunken Isle IPA: An off-white head sits atop an attractive amber beer. The aroma is a complex mix of hops and malt with traces of yeast. Assertively spicy hops balanced by a rich malt profile will entice the pallet. The finish is long with lingering hop bitterness. 6.8% ABV, 63 IBUs. Draft or cans.

Breakfast Beer: This started as a "one-off" in the fall of 2009, but was so instantly and immensely popular that it quickly became one of the brewery's mainstays. Its name is a bit of a joke, since its ingredients include two classic breakfast foods, milk (sugar) and oats. The beer is a hybrid of two classic stout styles; **oatmeal stouts**, which have oats added to the mash to increase the body and mouthfeel of the brew and **sweet or "milk" stouts**, which have unfermentable lactose (AKA milk sugar) added. Putting the two ideas together produced a stout that to look at is absolutely opaque, with a nice tan head. The aroma speaks strongly of roasted grains, as you would expect from a stout, while on the tongue the beer has tremendous body. There is a decided silkiness on the palate from the oats, combined with mild sweetness from the lactose and roasted flavors from the grains. Hops are there strictly for balance, with no noticeable presence. An unusual but excellent beer. 4.9% ABV, 26 IBUs. Draft only at present, but likely this will be the next beer added to the can line-up.

Honeymoon Hefe: A true marriage between German and American styles. Light and refreshingly made with 45% wheat malt, then cleanly fermented to yield a crisp, almost pilsner-like beer that is refreshing, somewhat fruity, and ideal for a summer's afternoon. 5.2% ABV, 25 IBUs. Draft only.

Peninsula Brewers Reserve (PBR): A light, straw-colored ale with a fresh, clean aroma and very subtle hops. Crisp in the taste with a slight fruitiness. Finishes dry and refreshing. 5.2% ABV, 15 IBUs. Draft only.

Naptown Brown Ale: A "nut" brown in the literal sense – with an ample supply of toasted pecans added to the mash during the brew! Plenty of malt and roasted grains hit the palate with a hint of chocolate and coffee backed up with nice hop bitterness. 6.3% ABV, 40 IBUs. Draft only.

Arctic XPA: An American-Style Pale Ale with an extra hop kick! A crisp, quenching ale with hints of grapefruit in the bitterness. A little malted oats added to the mix lends a nice texture and balance to all that hoppy goodness! 5.2% ABV, 72 IBUs. Draft only.

Special/Seasonal Offerings

Winter Warlock Old Ale: A delicious English-style Old Ale brewed each fall and then conditioned for nearly a year. It's tapped each October 1st, an event which is eagerly anticipated by local craft beer lovers. The long conditioning period produces a wonderfully rich flavor profile. 9.2% ABV, 67 IBUs. Draft only.

Single Hop IPAs: Kenai River Brewing offers these beers on an irregular basis, depending on hop availability and their brewing schedule. They are very similar to their flagship **Sunken Isle IPA**, except that only a single hop variety is used. 7.2% ABV, 70 IBUs. Draft only.

Distribution and Availability

Besides the brewery, Kenai River Brewing self-distributes to several restaurants and bars with the Kenai-Soldotna area. Beyond the local area, their beers are distributed by Specialty Imports throughout the Peninsula and to several areas of the state, including Anchorage, Fairbanks and Juneau. As of this writing, their beers are not yet available outside of Alaska.

Kassik's Brewery

Location:

47160 Spruce Haven St.

Kenai, AK 99611

Phone: 907-776-4055

Email: info@kassiksbrew.com

Website: www.kassiksbrew.com

Hours of Operation:

Winter Hours: Tuesday - Saturday: 12:00 - 7:00 pm. Sunday: 12:00 - 5:00. Monday: CLOSED.

Summer Hours (May – August): Monday - Saturday 12:00 - 7:00 pm. Sunday 12:00 - 5:00 pm.

Driving Directions: Drive north out of the city of Kenai to Mile 19.1 of the Kenai Spur Hwy. Take a right on South Miller Loop. Follow the road as it eventually makes a turn to the left, and then take right on to Holt-Lamplight at the Stop-N-Go. Take a left on Spruce Haven St, and the brewery will be on the right. Watch for blue signs by the roadside pointing the way.

Overview

Kassik's Brewery is the Kenai Peninsula's version of a traditional farmhouse brewery. Its story began with the gift of a homebrewing kit from Debbie Kassik to her husband Frank for Christmas. Frank rapidly became a proficient homebrewer, and then the couple began to consider the possibility of opening a commercial brewery. First, they constructed a 36' x 50' shed next to their home, and then in May 2005 they purchased a used brewhouse. They remodeled the building to accommodate it, with the help of family and friends. On Memorial Day in 2006, they opened for business as Kassik's Kenai Brew Stop.

In the years since that opening, Kassik's Brewery has been a big success. They changed their name after a few years to eliminate customer confusion between themselves and Kenai River Brewing Company. Word of mouth regarding the excellent beers they were producing quickly spread around the peninsula and the state. Demand for their brews was so great that in 2010 they completed a major expansion, basically tripling their square footage, adding a great deal more tank space and a bottling line, plus a brand new tasting room. Today, besides Frank, Debbie and their sons are deeply involved in running the brewery

Brewery Characteristics

The brewhouse of Kassik's Brewery is a 7-barrel system, purchased from Alice's Champagne Palace in Homer, which had a short run as a brewpub before reverting to its current status as just a bar. Fermentation at Kassik's has always been closed, initially using Grundy tanks before adding larger conical fermenters.

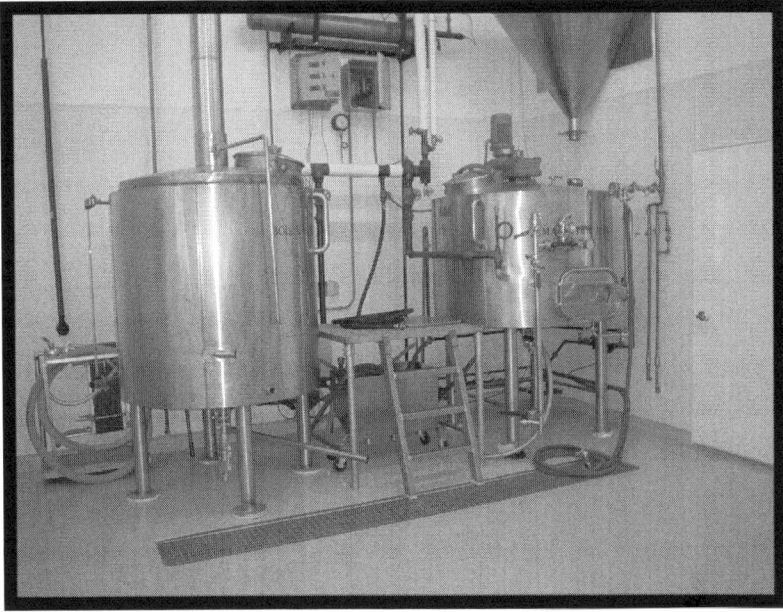

Kassik's Brew Kettle & Mash Tun

Initially their beers were only available on draft, but with the expansion in 2010, Kassik's began moving into bottling. Some of their bottled beers are filtered and force carbonated, while others are bottled conditioned.

The tasting room at Kassik's Brewery has ten taps, with plastic party pigs and 64-oz. growlers available, as well as a cooler with a good selection of their bottled beers. There is no food available.

The Brewer Speaks

Owner/Brewer Frank Kassik in his own words:

How did you become a commercial brewer?

"Starting out in the world of craft brewing for me was a complete accident. I was working for Agrium at the time, they were starting to spread rumors of closing the facility and I threw out the idea of opening a brewery. Everything started snowballing into a blur of stainless and piping to where we are today."

What do you see as the biggest challenges facing a craft brewer in Alaska?

"Shipping in or throughout this state has to be our biggest challenge. Pretty much all of our raw materials have to be brought up by barge to Anchorage then trucked down the peninsula. Getting our product out to our consumers is also a huge undertaking with being the largest state in the union with only 722,000 people. Our nearest large towns are three and seven hours away from us."

What characteristics do you think define Alaska craft beer, as opposed to craft beer brewed elsewhere?

"Defining Alaska craft beer is easy, community. Although we are in the largest state, there doesn't seem anywhere we can't go without seeing someone we know or they recognize us. It's almost uncanny how quickly our name has become known and how many friends have been made on our journeys."

Where do you think Alaska craft brewing in general and your brewery/brewpub in particular will be in eight to ten years?

"I have been shooting from the hip since the beginning, our growth rate is still overwhelming, but we're having a lot of fun. I don't plan on changing the pattern anytime soon."

The Beers

Regularly On-Tap

Note: All of Kassik's standard beers are available on draft and in 22 oz. bottles.

Whalers Wheat: An American Style Hefeweizen that has little to no hop flavor with a hint of citrus. 5% ABV.

Orion's Quest Red Ale: A bold red ale, this beer is malt forward but with enough hops for good balance. It was created to honor the Chief Petty Officers of the United States Navy. 6.8% ABV.

Beaver Tail Blonde: This blonde ale has a pleasant light spicy hop flavor that balances with a hint of sweet malt flavor. 5.2% ABV.

Dolly Varden Nut Brown: A delicious nut brown ale with wonderful malt flavors. Good balance of chocolate, caramel sweetness and a modest nutty flavor up front. Some dark toast and slight hop profile in the background. 5.5% ABV. There is also an imperial version, called *Big Nutz Imperial Brown Ale*, which earned a Gold Medal in the 2011 Tasting Institute's World Beer Championships.

Moose Point Porter: This porter has a dark and heavy appearance with a surprisingly light and clean finish. This beer took a Silver Medal at the 2011 World Beer Championship and a Bronze in 2008. 5.2% ABV.

Roughneck Stout: This beer has a bold taste of complex roasted malts with just the right amount of hops to balance things out. 7.2% ABV.

Pale Moon Pale Ale: A quenching, hop forward bouquet and clean finish make this an excellent example of the pale ale style. 6.4% ABV.

Morning Wood IPA: This beer is made is the style of English IPAs, so the bitterness is more restrained than is typical for an American IPA. However, the hops used are the more assertive Pacific Northwest varieties, producing a beer that straddles the style boundaries. Extremely drinkable and very popular. 6.4% ABV.

Serving bar in Kassik's Tasting Room

Special/Seasonal Offerings

Caribou Kilt Wee Heavy Scotch Ale: This beer is in the style known as "Scotch" or "Strong Scotch", and should not be confused with "Scottish" style ales, which are similar but not nearly so strong. Caribou Kilt weighs in at a hefty 8.5% ABV and is an outstanding example of the style, as evidenced by its winning a Bronze Medal at the 2008 World Beer Cup in San Diego. Available on draft and in bottles.

Double Wood Imperial IPA: The beer pours a dark gold, with a rocky, cream-colored head, long-lasting and producing extensive lacing. The aroma is of hops, hops, and more hops, as you'd expect in a 95 IBU beer. On the tongue, there is a long, deep hop flavor, extraordinarily well-balanced for the degree of bitterness. I've had beers that were actually hopped much less than this one which had a much harsher hop taste. When Frank Kassik selected the exact blend of hop varieties to use on this beer, I think he may have achieved perfection or something damn near. The finish is long and more-ish, the 9+% ABV notwithstanding. Available on draft.

Buffalo Head Barley Wine: The beer poured a lovely dark honey color in the glass, with a nice, dense cream-colored head. The aroma was rich with malty notes and a touch of alcohol. Very good mouthfeel, with plenty of complex, malty flavors from the deep malt backbone. With just enough hop bitterness for balance, this is definitely in the English rather than the American style. A long, slow finish with a little more alcohol heat completes the package. It's no wonder that Kassik's took a barley wine Gold Medal in the 2011 Tasting Institute's World Beer Championships. Available in bottles and on draft.

Smoked Russian Imperial Stout: It pours completely opaque with a nice tan head that dissipates to a collar and leaves good lacing on the glass. The aroma is just what you'd expect, being chock full of roasty, espresso notes, backed up with malty sweetness and a touch of smoke. On the palate it is rich and chewy, with lots of mouthfeel. Flavors of roasted malt, smoke, and coffee intertwine in a complex dance on your tongue. The finish is nice and warming. If you're a fan of smoked beers or imperial stouts, you really need to give this one a try. This beer also took a Gold Medal in the Tasting Institute's World Beer Championships. Available on draft or in bottles.

Imperial Spiced Honey Wheat: At 8.9% ABV, this is no summer-time light-weight wheat beer! It's a great sipping beer to enjoy by the fire and help ward off the winter chill. Available on draft.

Distribution and Availability

Besides the brewery, Kassik's Brewery self-distributes to several restaurants and bars with the Kenai-Soldotna area. Beyond the local area, their beers are distributed by Odom Distributors throughout the Peninsula and to several areas of the state, including Anchorage, Fairbanks and Juneau. Additionally, bottled versions of some of their beers are now available in the Seattle area.

Homer Brewing Company

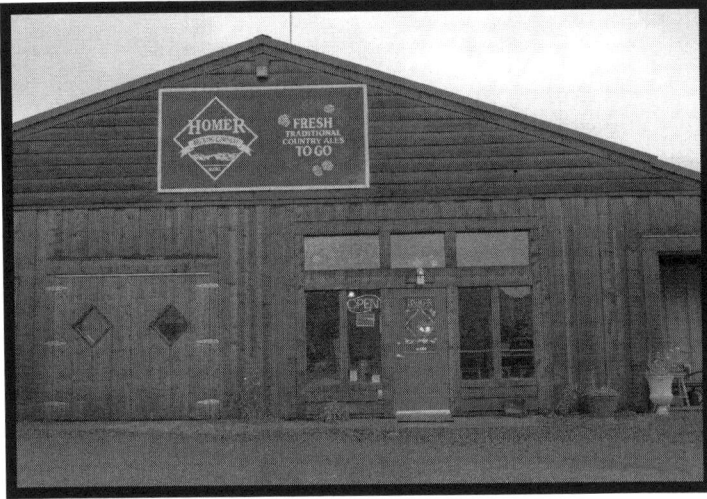

Location:

1411 Lake Shore Dr.

Homer, AK 99603

Phone: 907-235-3626

Email: mailto:info@homerbrew.com

Website: http://www.homerbrew.com

Hours of Operation:

Summer hours: 12 to 7 PM, Monday – Saturday, 12 to 6 PM Sunday.

Winter hours: 12 to 6 PM, Monday-Saturday, 12 to 5 PM Sunday.

Driving Directions: Follow the Sterling Highway south to Homer. After you pass Beluga Lake on your left, the highway will turn left and become Ocean Drive. Take the second left, onto Douglas Place. Take a right onto Lake Shore Drive. The brewery will be on the right.

Overview

In 1996 three people -- Steve McCasland, Lasse Holmes & Karen Berger – decided to open Homer's first commercial brewery, which was also the first craft brewery on the Kenai Peninsula. On September 21, 1996, Homer Brewing opened its doors in a 23' by 29' space, using a cobbled-together 3-barrel brewhouse. Over the next five years, Homer Brewing grew to produce over 1000 barrels per year using this small system.

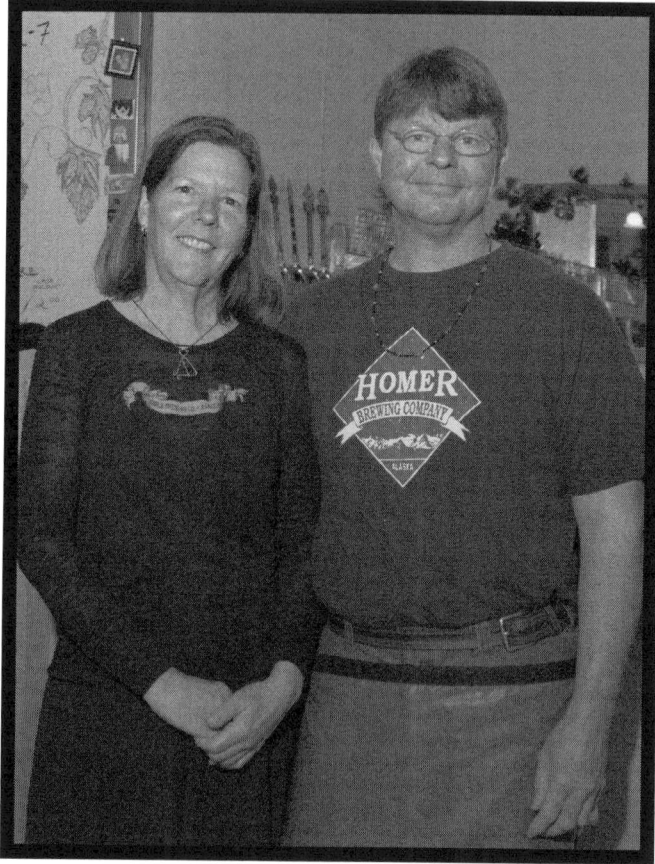

Karen Berger and Steve McCasland

In February 2001, Homer Brewing purchased their current location as a permanent home for the brewery. In May of 2005, they expanded their production capacity by installing their current brewhouse. Today, Karen and Steve continue the good work of supplying the people of Homer with craft beer.

Brewery Characteristics

Homer Brewing uses a 6-barrel brewhouse. Due to the open layout of the brewery, the production area is totally visible from the retail sales area.

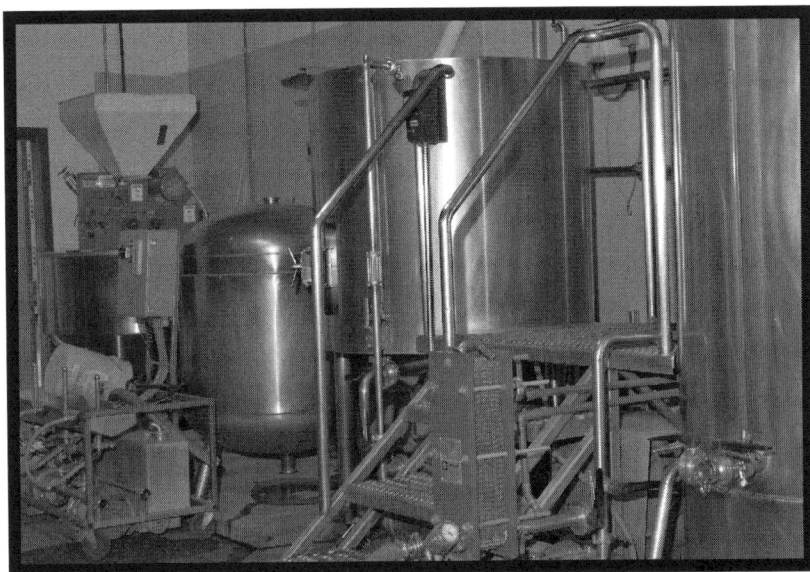

Homer Brewing's 6-barrel brewhouse

Homer Brewing prides itself on offering "Fresh, Traditional Country Ales to go," with all of their beers being cask-conditioned and non-pasteurized, so they are exclusively focused on growler sales and local taps. They have a small tasting area and there are also picnic tables and a gazebo set up outside the brewery to create an impromptu beer garden.

Homer's retail area. The brewhouse is off camera to the left.

The Brewer Speaks

Owner/Brewers Karen Berger & Steve McCasland in their own words.

How did you become a commercial brewer?

"Homer Brewing Company came to be from a combined vision of the desire to live in Homer, create an income and for the love of beer. The Q & Q (Quality and Quaffability) homebrew club here in Homer that spawned several of Alaska's present-day professional brewers was the basis of brewing education. The timing of the mid 90s was an era of Alaska craft brewery openings that set the foundation (and the bar) for Alaska's beer culture. We felt sure if there was a brewery in Homer, our efforts would be supported by the community. The "commercial brewer", in reality is 2 people and 2 distinct jobs at Homer Brewing Company. Karen is all things administrative and Steve is all things brewing. Together we are commercial brewers."

What do you see as the biggest challenges facing a craft brewer in Alaska?

"The obvious challenge we face is that of transportation. The rising costs and fragility of the system makes our remote location precarious for obtaining ingredients and goods. Outside crop failure is also a factor. With the boom in Alaska's agricultural diversity, it would be good to see growth in barley acreage with a malting facility added within the state. Hops cannot be grown at our latitudes in an open field, but the use of the high tunnels that are being made available to farmers; it could be possible to make a dent in hop usage at the local level. The other most inhibiting factor to breweries in Alaska is the statutes that impede individual business freedom."

What characteristics do you think define Alaska craft beer, as opposed to craft beer brewed elsewhere?

"Diversity in a small market. From very local breweries like Homer to a regional brewery like Alaskan with the gumbo of styles, both in beer and business models, to choose from."

Where do you think Alaska craft brewing in general and your brewery/brewpub in particular will be in eight to ten years?

"The maturation of some, growth of others, emergence of new ideas and steady industry growth will continue to enhance Alaska's breweries. As for Homer Brewing Company, we are at our zenith at this writing. We plan to age gracefully with the business of being HOMER'S brewing company and being a strong thread in the fabric of our community. We are honored to be the first brewery on the Kenai Peninsula and hope to maintain our steady course and welcome those that come to visit our incredible area. We would like to think by that 10 year mark, we have a different angle of vision answering these questions."

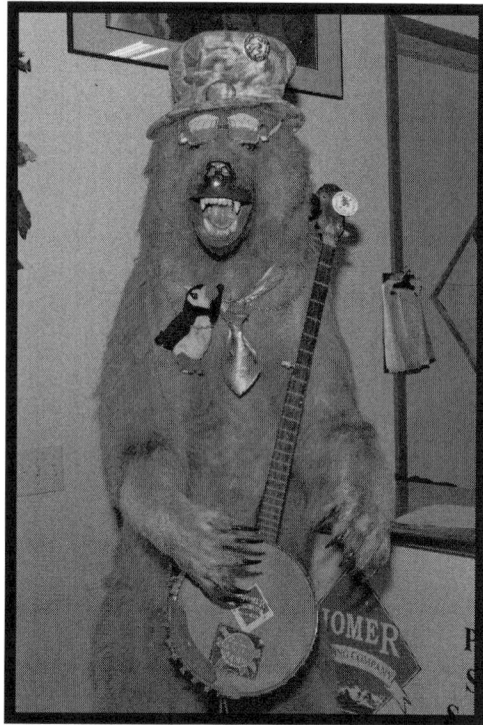

Homer Brewing Company's mascot

The Beers

Regularly On-Tap

Old Inlet Pale Ale: An American-style pale ale with hints of fruit and flowers from Cascade hops. ABV 5%.

Broken Birch Bitter: A Best Bitter with the bold, citrus-like flavors of Centennial and Cascade hops. Each keg is dry-hopped to give the additional nose that will satisfy any hop-head. This is very much a "session beer," with an ABV of around 5%. It is truly the signature beer of the brewmaster.

Red Knot Scottish: Named for a migrating shorebird. Using flavorful Scottish ale yeast and cask conditioning makes for an amber-colored, malty-sweet, "user-friendly" ale. Red Knot is very popular and is their #1 selling beer. ABV 5.6%.

China Poot Porter: Named for a particularly recognizable peak across Kachemak Bay, this porter is robust and flavorful from roasted malts, while slightly dry and crisp. ABV 5.4%.

Odyssey Oatmeal Stout: Homer's own "Iliad and Odyssey." This is a full-bodied stout that uses Scottish yeast and 12% oatmeal in the mash, giving it smooth flavor and rich body. ABV 6%.

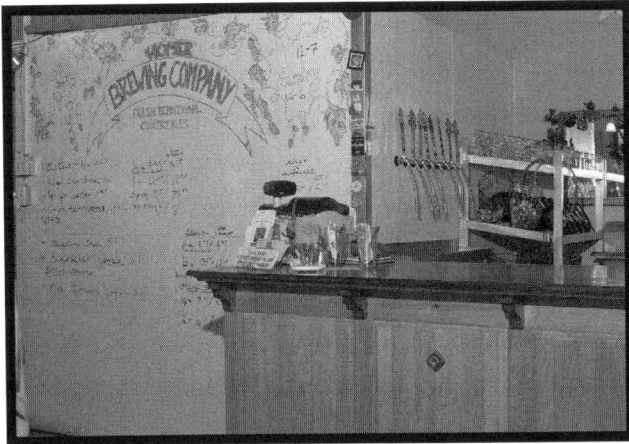

Serving counter at Homer Brewing

Special/Seasonal Offerings

Oktoberfest: Brewed with a California Common lager yeast, this Marzen is as close to a lager as Homer gets. Often, this yeast spawns other brews such as Harvest Rye Lager and Homer Dunkel. The flavors of fall.

Celestiale: A Belgian style spiced ale arrives around the Winter Solstice. This is the only beer that is conventionally bottled by the brewery. Limited to about 144 hand filled, hand numbered 22-ounce bottles, this is one you can cellar or enjoy during the holidays. ABV 6.7%.

Royal Imperial Stout: You know winter is here when this beer goes on tap. It's big, bold and will warm the cockles of your heart.

Distribution and Availability

Homer Brewing Company self-distributes their beers to many of the restaurants and bars in the Homer area. Fresh-filled growlers can also be purchased at the Fritz Creek General Store and at The Grog Shop on Pioneer Ave in Homer. The occasional keg will appear at the growler bars of La Bodega or Brown Jug Warehouse in Anchorage. However, all of Homer Brewing's beers are unpasteurized and cask-conditioned. With the delicate balance in each keg, being able to attend to any variances can only be done if they remain in the local market, so you will likely have to travel to Homer to experience these excellent beers.

Kodiak Island Brewing Company

Location:

117 Lower Mill Bay Rd.

Kodiak, AK 99615

Phone: 907-486-ALES (2537)

Email: bmills@ak.net

Website: http://www.kodiakbrewery.com

Hours of Operation:

12 to 7 PM, seven days a week.

Driving Directions: Kodiak Island Brewing Company is located in the center of town, near the intersection of Lower Mill Bay Road and Rezanof Drive. It is right next to a McDonalds.

Overview

Kodiak Island Brewing Company was established by Ben Millstein. A carpenter by trade and avid homebrewer, Millstein spent several years in Homer and was a member of the local homebrew club and friends with Lasse Holmes, Steve McCasland, and Karen Berger, who eventually founded Homer Brewing Company in 1996. Inspired by their example, he decided to open a brewery on Kodiak Island in 2003. Nine years and a great deal of hard work later, Kodiak Island Brewing Company has been quite successful, and in August 2012 completed a move from its small original location to a new and much larger home on Lower Mill Bay Road.

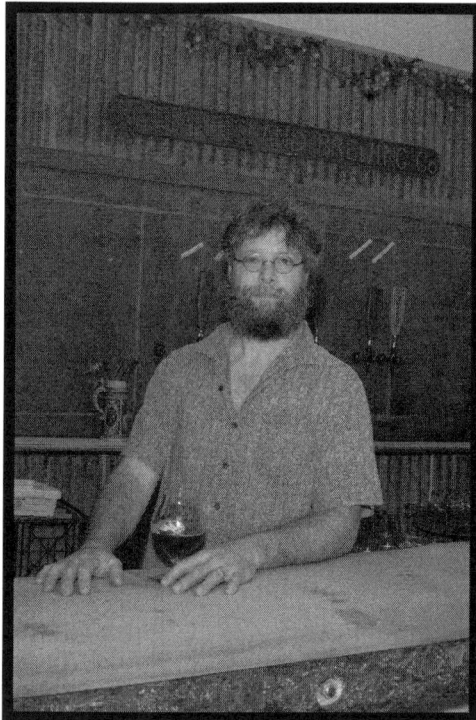

Ben Millstein, Owner & Brewer

Given its remote location, Kodiak Island Brewing brews beers aimed squarely at the local market. They are the second largest consumer of Quoin Beer Pigs in the country, as this is a favorite way for the locals to take their brews home. The last nine years have built up a great bond of trust between the brewery and the people of Kodiak, which now allows Millstein the freedom to brew the occasional "palate-expanding" experiment. Looking ahead, he has voiced a desire to begin limited experiments in barrel-aged beers. He has also ordered two tanks for aging with *brettanomyces* yeast.

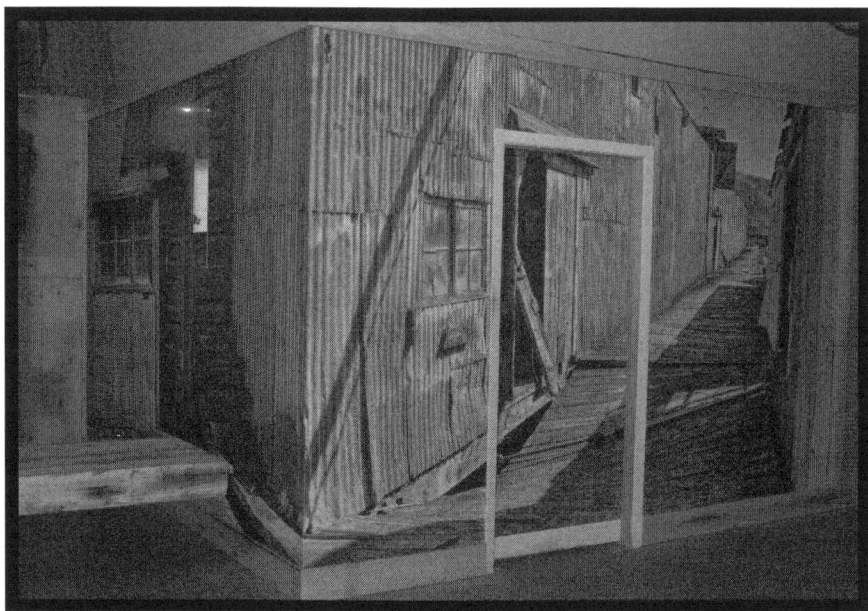

Tap Room Mural

Brewery Characteristics

The brewhouse at Kodiak Island is a 10-barrel system that was originally built for the Hop Cats Brewery in Chicago. Fermentation is closed, using conical fermenters. Production capacity was recently increased by the addition of three new tanks, a 30-barrel fermenter and two 30-barrel conditioning tanks.

Fermenters in Kodiak Island's fermenters

Kodiak Island's recent move increased its overall floor space from 2400 to 9000 square feet. Besides the increased number of tanks, this move also tripled the size of the tap room. The new tap room is open and airy, with many pieces of local memorabilia and repurposed items.

Filling a growler at the brewery tap

Pigs waiting for pick-up

The tap room can have up to nine beers on at any one time. Plastic pigs and 64-oz. growlers (both glass and stainless steel) are available.

A tap room counter, supported by masts from old boats

The Brewer Speaks

Owner/Brewer Ben Millstein in his own words:

How did you become a commercial brewer?

"Force of will and community need."

What do you see as the biggest challenges facing a craft brewer in Alaska?

"One of the cool things about brewing is that there are such variable challenges. But for a brewer in Alaska particularly I guess shipping and planning ahead are the big ones. That's really true for a lot of businesses in the state though. Another challenge is maintaining connections to the larger national scene I suppose. But you can decide to what degree that's important for you. Our remoteness probably makes Craft Brewer Conferences, collaboration projects, and other events that much more fun and worthwhile."

What characteristics do you think define Alaskan craft beer, as opposed to craft beer brewed elsewhere?

"The main thing I think of is the barley wine theme encouraged by the annual festival along with the climate. That's not too unusual though, I don't think. There are other areas where strong beers are emphasized as at least an omnipresent part of the portfolio like San Diego, or Colorado. Maybe another characteristic would be Alaskan rugged independence. People here seem to like to figure things out a lot themselves rather than hiring someone."

Where do you think Alaskan craft brewing in general and your brewery/brewpub in particular will be in eight to ten years?

"I've been so busy and focused on getting where I am I haven't put a lot of thought in what's to come after. I do know that as an industry segment, we're in a period of unprecedented and explosive growth. I think there's still a lot of room for small, local operations like ours; what I call the bakery model, or for brewpubs. I'm afraid we might see another "shake out" like we saw in the late '90s of distributing breweries. There's only so much space on the liquor store shelves."

"For our operation I hope to be able to add more specialty beers. We haven't had the space in the past, to do as many as I'd like, but I think we do now if we can make the time. I don't have any plans to distribute or package, or add food, about which I am asked every day."

The Beers

Regularly on-Tap

Wing-Nut Brown Ale: A robust and hoppy brown ale, at 5% ABV.

North Pacific Ale: More or less in the style of a Scottish ale, this 4.5% ABV brew pours a dark caramel color with a small tan head. The nose is of malt & caramel, with the tiniest hint of roast. Excellent mouthfeel, good carbonation, very malt forward, with a nice, clean taste. Extremely drinkable, an excellent session beer.

Liquid Sunshine: One of their flagship brews, this is a classic California Common or Steam beer. It is a deep golden color in the glass, with a very nice white head that left excellent lacing on the glass. Great carbonation, and clean, crisp hoppiness, falling off to a nice finish. Extremely drinkable at 5% ABV, it is easy to see why this beer is such a big seller.

Sarah Pale Blonde Ale: Named after a certain former governor of this fair state, this is a 5% ABV coastal lager or steam beer. While this beer is touted as "Great body, no head" like its namesake, in reality it pours a dark gold with a nice white head. The aroma is primarily of malt, as is the flavor profile.

Snowshoe Pale Ale: This beer is aggressively dry-hopped with Amarillo hop. Coming in at about 4.2% ABV, it's an excellent session beer for the hop lover.

Special/Seasonal Offerings

Kodiak Island Brewing Company typically has four specialty brews on at any time, since they have nine taps. These beers will typically include a stout of some sort, and often a wheat beer, fruit beer, or strong beer. Below are a couple of examples of the over thirty different beers that they have offered at one time or another.

Devil's Club Strong Ale: This beer was created by Brewer Mike Trussell; rumor has it he wanted to convey what it feels like to be hit in the face with Devil's Club. (For those of you non-Alaskans out there, Devil's Club, scientific name *Opolpanax horridus*, is a plant covered in very nasty, tiny brittle spines.) It's a brew that reminds me a bit of **Stone Brewing's** *Arrogant Bastard Ale*, being strong (8%) and very hoppy. It pours a very dark honey color with a small head. The aroma is full of Simcoe hop aroma, and on the tongue there is great balance between the massive malt backbone and the ton of hop bitterness and flavor. A great brew, but definitely not one you could have more than one of!

Bering Sea Scotch Ale: This beer pours a dark, semi-translucent ruby, with a nice off-white head. The smoked malt used makes its presence known with authority in the nose. There is excellent body to the beer, a real sturdy malt forward flavor profile, plus the nice smoke flavors, all dropping off to an excellent finish.

Distribution and Availability

Besides the brewery, Kodiak Island Brewing Company self-distributes their beers to many of the restaurants and bars on Kodiak. Unfortunately, their beers are seldom available anywhere else. The occasional keg will appear at Café Amsterdam or Humpy's Alehouse in Anchorage and the brewery is usually represented at the Great Alaskan Beer and Barley Wine Festival, held each January in Anchorage. Barring these rare appearances, you will have to travel to Kodiak Island to experience these excellent beers.

Seward Brewing Company

Location:

139 4th Ave.

Seward, AK 99664

Phone: 907-422-0337

Email: mail@sewardbrewing.com

Website: http://www.sewardbrewingcompany.com/

Hours of Operation:

4 to 10 PM, seven days a week.

Driving Directions: Drive south on the Seward Highway to Seward. The Seward Highway will become 3rd Ave in the downtown area. The Seward Brewing Company is located one block north of the Alaska SeaLife Center, on the corner of 4th Ave and Washington St.

Overview

The Seward Brewing Company is the new kid on the block on the Kenai Peninsula, having only opened for business on August 17th, 2012. It is housed in a historic building, dating from the 1940s, which was originally a mercantile store with offices upstairs. Most recently, the 13,500-square-foot building served as the Seward Elk's Lodge, before being purchased by local businessman Gene Minden and extensively renovated. Now the building boasts a bar on the main floor, along with the brewery and retail store, a restaurant upstairs with magnificent views of Resurrection Bay and the surrounding mountains, and private meeting/dining rooms in the basement. Currently, the brew master at Seward Brewing Company is Kevin Burton, who also fills that role at Glacier Brewhouse in Anchorage.

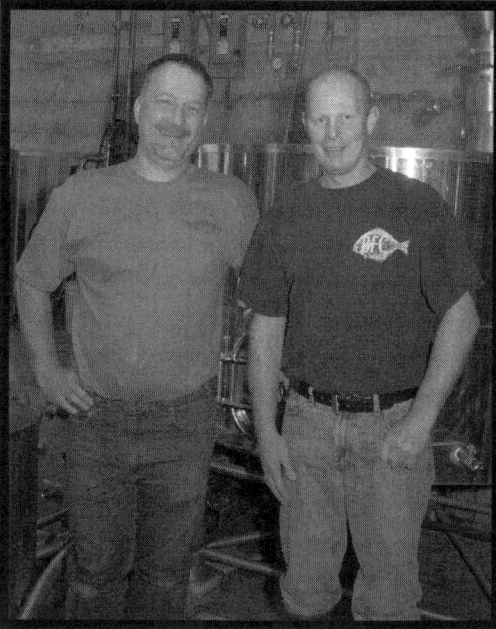

SBC Owner Gene Minden and Brewer Kevin Burton

Brewery Characteristics

The brewhouse at the Seward Brewing Company has an interesting history. For years the 8.5-barrel steam-fired brewhouse stood idle in the front window of another Seward establishment, Chinooks Restaurant at the Seward Boat Harbor. That restaurant was also owned at that time by Gene Minden, the current owner of the Seward Brewing Company, and he had always intended for it to be a brewpub. For various reasons, those plans never came to fruition, so when the opportunity arose for him to sell Chinooks and open SBC, he took the brewhouse with him. Now it has a new home and is producing beers under the skillful guidance of Kevin Burton.

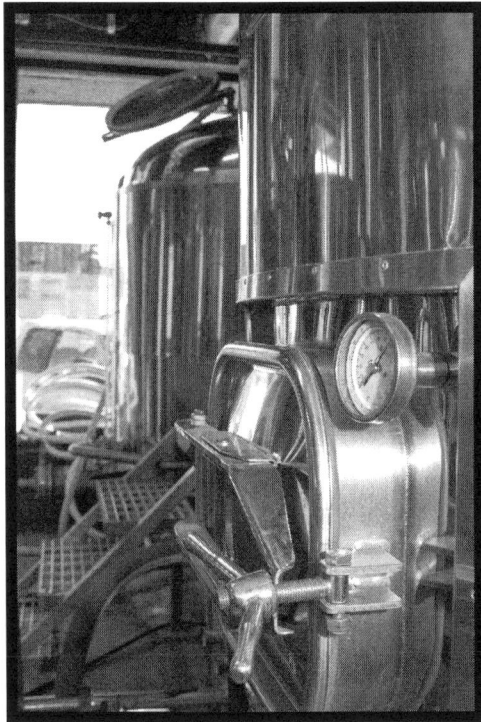

Passers-by on 4ᵗʰ Ave have a nice view of SBC's copper brewkettle

The initial offerings have been in styles which are easily recognized by the general public. Beers are fermented in closed conical fermenters. Since the brewpub has opened fairly recently, it remains to be seen what sort of distinctive house character may develop for its beers. Besides their own brews, SBC also offers a nice selection of other local craft beers, including the occasional Rough Draft experimental beer from Alaskan Brewing Company.

Restaurant Menu

The food at the Seward Brewing Company could be described as typical pub/bar fare, but with a gourmet twist. There are plenty of good appetizers, like nachos, hot wings and beer-batter fried cheese curds, but the nachos, for example, are made with goat cheese and smoked bacon. There's also an excellent beer and cheese soup, made using their own Red Ale.

For entrees, besides the several different burger options, they also offer steaks, BBQ ribs, and several dishes highlighting the amazing local Alaskan seafood, such as halibut, salmon, and king crab. Clearly at the Seward Brewing Company, the food is just as important as the beer.

The Brewer Speaks

SBC Brewer Kevin Burton in his own words:

How did you become a commercial brewer?

"Hard work, apprenticeships, and formal brewing education at the Seibel Institute in Chicago, Illinois. And more hard work."

What do you see as the biggest challenges facing a craft brewer in Alaska?

"Infrastructure for brewery utilities and brewer education opportunities."

What characteristics do you think define Alaska craft beer, as opposed to craft beer brewed elsewhere?

"The water. Cold weather."

Where do you think Alaska craft brewing in general and your brewery/brewpub in particular will be in eight to ten years?

"There is a glut of breweries right now just as in the 1990s. Some will survive and some will not. The difference now being that the beer is better quality. In the 90s, breweries failed due to bad beer and/or bad business practices. Today, most of those without business acumen will probably fail. It is much more of a competitive environment now. As for us, continued successful growth is predicted for the next ten years."

The Beers

Regularly on-Tap

Seward Golden Ale: The semi-obligatory transition beer, designed not to scare off the novice craft beer drinker. Light colored, light bodied, hopped with restraint, smooth to drink. Inoffensive. 4.63% ABV.

Seward IPA: Pours a light honey color, with a small, off-white head. The nose is laced with the characteristic aroma of Cascade hops, which are used in the dry hopping. On the tongue there is good bitterness, and nice, clean flavors. Overall, a very respectable example of the style. 5.9% ABV.

Seward Red Ale: The beer is a dark honey or caramel color, and had little in the way of head. The aroma makes it clear that this is a malt forward beer. In the mouth the malt leads the charge, but there are enough hops for balance. Very drinkable and an excellent accompaniment to their food. 6.2% ABV.

Seward White Ale: An American style wheat beer. Its aroma shows the use of spices. Look for hints of chamomile and coriander, as well as sweet and bitter orange peels in both the nose and flavor profile. 4.7% ABV.

Seward Oatmeal Stout: The newest addition to SBC's line-up, this is a classic oatmeal stout, with plenty of dark, roasted barley flavors, plus the silkiness on the palate from the addition of oats to the mash. Delicious!

Specialty/Seasonal Offerings

The Seward Brewing Company has not yet offered any special or seasonal offerings.

Distribution and Availability

Because the Seward Brewing Company is licensed as a brewpub, Alaska law prohibits them from packaging or distributing their beers. Beers are typically available by the glass or by the growler (32- or 64-oz. size). You might also encounter their brews at various beer festivals around the state.

St. Elias Brewing Company

Location:

434 Sharkathmi Ave.

Soldotna, AK 99669

Phone: 907-260-7837

Email: steliasbrewing@live.com

Website: www.steliasbrewingco.com

Hours of Operation:

Summer hours: 12 to 10 PM, Sunday thru Thursday. 12 to 11 PM, Friday & Saturday

Winter hours: 12 to 9 PM, Sunday thru Thursday. 12 to 10 PM Friday & Saturday.

Driving Directions: Heading into Soldotna from the east on the Sterling Highway, St. Elias is visible on your left. Take a left onto Sharkathmi Avenue. Heading into Soldotna from the west, you will drive through town, and then, after passing Fred Meyer on your right, take a right onto Sharkathmi Avenue.

Overview

When Zach Henry and his family returned to his boyhood home of Soldotna in 2006 after a sojourn in the Lower 48, it was his intention to open a packaging brewery. He had acquired the necessary skill through both formal education and through working at the Yazoo Brewing Company in Nashville, Tennessee. However, he soon learned that not one but two such breweries (Kenai River Brewing and Kassik's Brewery) were in the process of opening in the Kenai/Soldotna area. Rather than go head-to-head with them as the newcomer, Henry decided to shift gears and open a brewpub. Being a hands-on sort of fellow, he and his father did much of the construction of the brewpub themselves, finally opening for business in May 2008, just in time for the busy tourist season. The brewpub is a true family affair, with Henry's sister, Jessie Henry-Kolesar, overseeing the food service, while he focuses primarily on brewing.

Since St. Elias opened for business two years after the two other craft breweries in the Central Peninsula, it was able to build on the initial work those breweries had done in educating the local beer palate. It was also able to capitalize on the local demand for a pleasant place to enjoy good food and excellent beer. The depth of this demand became apparent in the fall and winter of 2008, after the always-busy tourist season concluded. Henry had planned to operate reduced hours during the winter, opening perhaps only three or four days a week, expecting a big fall-off in demand. Instead, St. Elias remained busy enough to stay open seven days a week, even during the depth of winter, thanks to the loyalty and enthusiasm of local residents.

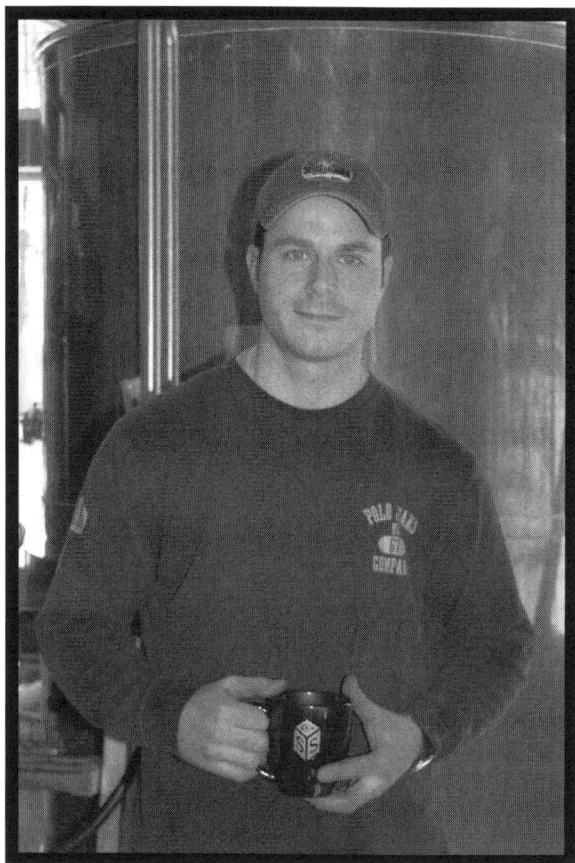

Owner/brewer Zach Henry

Brewery Characteristics

The heart of St. Elias is a steam-fired, 7-barrel system, originally built for the John Harvard's Brewhouse brewpub in Cambridge, Massachusetts. Fermentation takes place primarily in closed, conical fermenters, though there is also an extensive barrel-aging program. Henry makes frequent use of both used whiskey and wine barrels for aging certain of his brews.

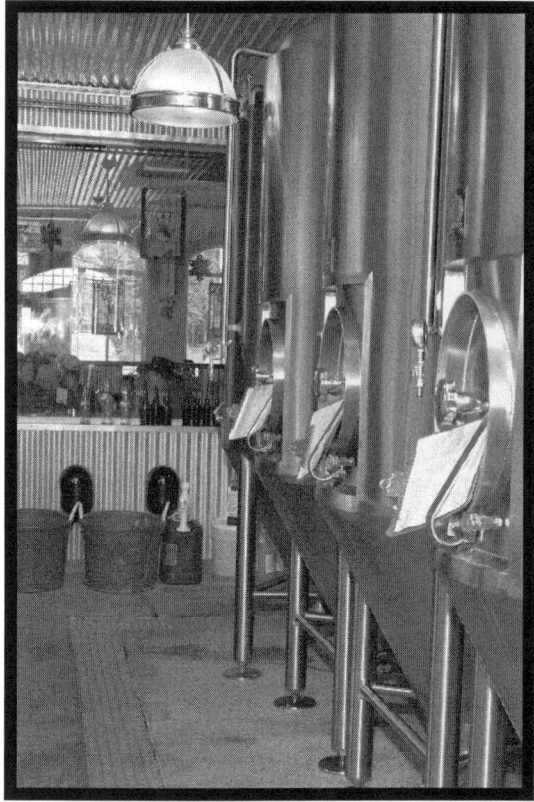

St. Elias fermenters look out onto the dining room

In June of 2010, Henry took the next logical step and began serving cask-conditioned beers for special events, such as the First Friday of each month. Initially these beers were tapped and served via gravity from the bar top, but in December 2011 St. Elias installed a true British-style beer engine, the first of its kind on the Peninsula. Cask availability is intermittent, so be sure to ask your server.

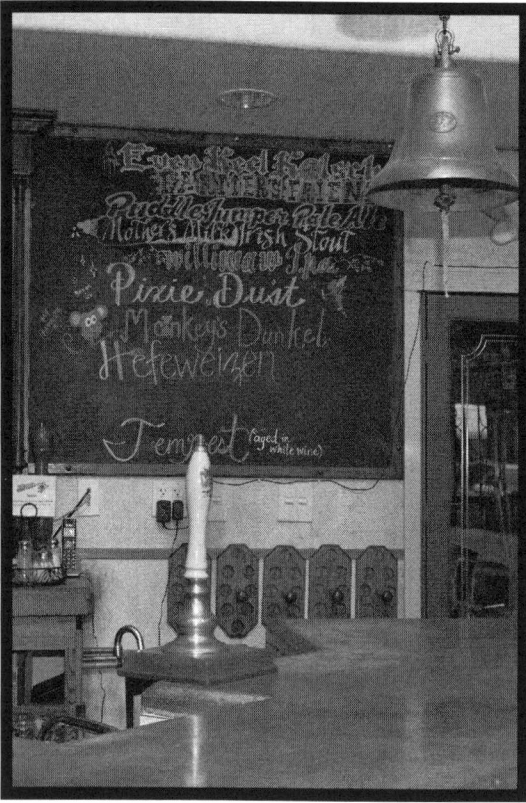

The only cask ale hand pump on the Peninsula

The defining characteristic of many of St. Elias' beers is the use of barrel aging. Beginning in April 2009 with one whiskey barrel that he brought back with him from the Lower 48, Henry has gradually expanded his barrel collection to the point where it now exceeds 24 barrels. Besides bourbon and rye whiskey barrels, Henry has also used brandy barrels and wine barrels, both red and white. The barrels are a mix of French, American, and Hungarian oak. Most recently, in the spring of 2012, he has begun to experiment with sour beers and beers which have undergone a secondary fermentation with *brettanomyces* yeast.

Just a few of St. Elias Brewing's barrels

Restaurant Menu

Besides the bar area, St. Elias can seat up to 100 patrons in booths and at tables, plus another 30 on an outside patio, weather permitting. The house specialty is 11" stone-fired rustic pizzas, prepared and baked in full view of the patrons in a brick-lined pizza oven.

You can build your own pizza, of course, but there are also ten different house specialty pizzas, including:

The Brewhouse: garlic oil, mozzarella, provolone, bacon, Italian sausage, pepperoni, marinated mushrooms, caramelized onions.

St. Elias Brewing's pizza oven

The Smokestack: house red sauce, mozzarella, provolone, bacon, kalamata olives, and fresh rosemary.

The Chicken Pesto: pesto, mozzarella, provolone, chicken, caramelized onions, marinated mushrooms, roasted tomatoes, fresh basil.

In addition to their selection of gourmet pizzas, St. Elias offers a substantial appetizer menu, a soup of the day, several salads, and a limited number of sandwiches. And don't miss their Mt. Redoubt dessert, a chocolate cake with a molten chocolate center.

The Brewer Speaks

Brewer/Owner Zach Henry in his own words:

How did you become a commercial brewer?

"Like many commercial brewers, I started off as an eager homebrewer. My first batch of beer was fermented with the help of my wife's bread yeast, added just for good measure. I cursed the instructions for not explaining what the words "hops", "malt" and "wort" meant, and my father-in-law and I bravely gutted the end result down. All the while I patted myself on the back as if I had just split my first atom after reading Einstein's memoir. Too often I cracked open a bottle of home brew that I had dreamed about for weeks with fireworks and lollipops dancing in my head only to meet failure. Once, I had a friend ask me to come over so we could quickly drink his homebrew that he found was infected. He had what looked like a jellyfish swimming in it. This boosted my self-confidence a little.

Ultimately, after numerous failed attempts, I took a break from homebrewing and my wife and I moved to Nashville, TN, where she attended college. There my interest was reignited after exposure to some of the best brewpubs I'd ever visited. At one particular brewpub, I remember looking through the glass into the brewery. I was in awe of all the mysterious equipment, as if I was a kid peeking into Willy Wonka's chocolate factory. That event started a snowball that forged a path toward a brewing career. I decided if I was going to do it, I would do it right and get a formal education. So, I enrolled in the American Brewers Guild's Intensive Science and Engineering program.

Midway through the program, I happened to be buying malt at a local homebrew store and stumbled upon the owner of a new Nashville startup, Yazoo Brewing Company. It turned out to be perfect timing as he had completed the same program. He wasn't ready to hire anyone, but I was eager to learn so I offered free labor in trade for education. He took my offer and shortly after I was hired on at Yazoo Brewing Company as their first employee. I agreed to a two year contract with Yazoo, with the dream of starting my own brewery back in my hometown of Soldotna, Alaska. I learned a vast amount from owner/brewmaster Linus Hall and am ever grateful that he gave me the chance to work for him. Even if I broke the corner of his newly poured cement bar with a broom handle, and tortured all of his future employees by dropping kernels of malt in their boots when they were busy cleaning the mash tun.

Eventually, we moved back to Soldotna, and in the spring of 2006 my Dad (Ron Henry) and I broke ground on St Elias Brewing Co. I ramped up my homebrewing and would spend hours making beer after long days building. I was brewing so often that I would literally taste, take notes, and then dump the batch just to make room for the next one. By the time we had completed construction, I had accumulated a good recipe stockpile to propel me through our first year of business. It was a long road with more roadblocks than we would ever have dreamed. But, looking back, I wouldn't trade those two years with my Dad for anything in the world. In May of 2008, we officially opened the doors of St. Elias Brewing Company."

What do you see as the biggest challenges facing a craft brewer in Alaska?

"We live in a very "seasonal" state. The winter months are steady with the locals, but during our short summer, our state explodes with tourists. Generally in these times, the brewpub is bustling and the brewery is nearing full capacity to keep up. A brewer has to be ready to go from a steady walk to a full out sprint to keep up with a sometimes unpredictably busy tourist season. Shipping up here can also add a bit of stress during the busy summer months. Freight always takes longer and costs more than the Lower 48. Whether it's a shipment of growlers or raw materials like hops or malt, there's always a bit more planning that has to take place far ahead of time. The last thing you want is to be out of growlers in the middle of July with droves of angry sunburnt fisherman giving you the evil eye."

What characteristics do you think define Alaska craft beer, as opposed to craft beer brewed elsewhere?

"In Alaska, it seems that we aren't afraid to venture outside of the norm when it comes to beer styles. We're a fearless bunch. There's a lot of experimentation, and you can find some pretty unique beers being produced in Alaska breweries. You can usually find one or more oak barrels filled with some sort of liquid alchemy in most Alaska breweries. The Great Alaska Beer and Barley Wine Festival held every year in Anchorage is the largest barley wine competition in the nation. Alaska breweries almost always place in the top 3, more often than not with a barrel aged beer."

Where do you think Alaska craft brewing in general and your brewery/brewpub in particular will be in eight to ten years?

"Alaska has an enormous amount of brewery/brewpubs compared to its population. We live in a very thirsty state. The fact that we all seem to be thriving with very few closures, tells me there's plenty of room for more. I think craft beer in Alaska and as a whole will see steady growth for a long time. We brewers are a tight knit group, all working toward the same goal: Convert one person at a time from mass market swill to flavorful craft beer."

"As for St. Elias Brewing Company, in eight to ten years I expect we'll grow to meet demand."

"Currently we are working toward positive changes in legislation. Every brewery in Alaska has the potential for growth if it weren't for such prohibitive legislation. Unfortunately, both brewery/brewpub growth and output are highly restricted and stifled by Alaska State laws. Breweries and brewpubs add a significant amount of jobs and tax revenue to our communities. As we grow, so does our need for raw materials and other services. All of this goes back into the economy, making it a win-win for everybody. We have the demand but not the legal ability to tap deeper into this market. There is no perfect system, but there are legislative models that work well in other states that benefit the consumers, brewery/brewpubs and governing bodies. In eight to ten years, we'd be happy if the state would loosen its grip on this bridled industry and allow us to expand our potential using a more modern template."

The Beers

St. Elias Brewing Company typically has ten beers on offer; five regular brews and five special/ seasonal offering. Certain popular seasonal beers are repeated each year, but there are also many unique brews that are only offered once.

Regularly On-Tap

Even Keel Kolsch: A well-balanced ale, fermented cool, showcasing light malt flavors and a delicate kiss of German noble hops. Typically the lightest beer on offer, it pairs well with salads or chicken. 5.2% ABV, 20 IBUs.

Mother's Milk Irish Stout: A dry Irish stout, this beer is dark and smooth. Chocolate flavors blend with hints of earthy English hop notes, from the traditional East Kent Goldings used. Brewed with both pale roasted barley and flaked barley, it pairs well with any chocolate dish. 3.8% ABV, 40 IBUs.

Puddle Jumper Pale Ale: A copper-colored pale ale in the American style, this beer features caramel flavors and an assertive but well-balanced Pacific Northwest hop finish. Brewed with pale, caramel, and Belgian malts, and hopped with classic American hops, it goes well any meat or tomato dish. 5.5% ABV, 40 IBUs.

Farmer's Friend: The use of rye in the mash adds a dry, fruity complexity to this brew. Very malt forward in its flavor profile, it is hopped just to balance using noble hops. Besides rye, flaked maize and Belgian malts are also used. It makes a fine accompaniment to any bacon or sausage dish. 6.5% ABV, 14 IBUs.

Williwaw IPA: Copper-colored. Nice head with good lacing. Nice aroma of citrusy American hops. Good mouthfeel, pleasant pucker, just a hint of alcohol. Smooth finish. Very drinkable, leaves you wanting a second round. A nicely balanced American IPA, with plenty of hop aroma and flavor. 6.7% ABV, 60 IBUs.

Some of the eclectic decor at St. Elias

Special/Seasonal Offerings

Sunfire Saison: Pours a hazy orange-honey color, with a nice head. The aroma is typical of a Belgian saison: earthy, spicy, maybe a little citrus, some hoppiness. On the palate, Sunfire is classic Belgian; it's spicy, a little bit tart, and a bit dry. Comparing it to a Saison Dupont, the stereotypical Belgian saison, Sunfire is not quite as dry and not as hoppy, but it's well within the style boundaries and delicious to boot. ABV is 6.4%, so it should be treated with respect.

Hefeweizen: Served during the summer in the traditional 20-oz. tall glass, this is a classic Bavarian Hefeweizen, full of banana and clove notes from the yeast used. Often paired on tap with its darker brother, The Monkey's Dunkel.

Island Girl Ale: This is a "no doubter" raspberry ale, and is a pretty shade of pink, or maybe rose, in color. Coming in at 5.5% ABV, the raspberry flavor is very much in the forefront, with a nice clean finish and not much bitterness. A popular summer beer, especially with the ladies.

Moose Juice Barley Wine: OG 1085, 93 IBUs. This brew was aged for several months in a Heaven Hill Bourbon cask. It pours a dark brown, with very little head. The aroma is of alcohol and dark fruit, with some light hop notes. On the palate it's heavy, malt forward but with plenty of hop bitterness to balance. Alcohol is noticeable, some slight bourbon flavors present. Then the wood begins to make its presence known, with vanilla and even coconut flavors kicking in. Finish is long and warming, enticing you to take another ship. A fine American barley wine, with a more restrained use of wood than some of St. Elias' earlier barrel-aged beers. This beer took second place in the barley wine category at the Great Alaskan Beer and Barley wine Festival in 2011.

Distribution and Availability

St. Elias Brewing Company is licensed as a brewpub, so Alaska law prohibits them from packaging or distributing their beers. Beers are typically available by the glass or by the growler (32- or 64-oz. size). By prior arrangement, you may be able to purchase a 2.25-gallon plastic pig or a 5-gallon keg. You might also encounter their brews at various beer festivals around the state.

Places to Find Craft Beer

Seward

Bars/Restaurants

Seward Alehouse

215 4th Avenue

(907) 224-2337.

Smoke free. No food served. Seven beer taps and full bar.

Yukon Bar

203 4th Avenue

(907) 224-3063

Smoking. No food served. Good beer selection and full bar. Frequent live music.

Chinooks Bar

1404 4th Ave

(907) 224-2207   **http://www.chinooksbar.com/**

Smoke free. Serves lunch and dinner. Located at the Seward Boat Harbor; excellent views. Full bar, a dozen taps pouring beers from Alaska, plus a selection of bottled beers.

Package/Liquor Stores

Sak Town Liquor Store

11912 Seward Highway

(907) 224-5907

Best selection of craft beers in Seward. Look for a growler bar in early 2013.

Cooper Landing

Bars/Restaurants

Sunrise Inn

Mile 43 Sterling Highway

(907) 595-1222   **http://www.alaskasunriseinn.com/**

Smoking. Food served. Local beers on tap.

Package/Liquor Stores

Wildman's

Mile 47.5 Sterling Highway

(907) 595-1456   **http://www.wildmans.org/**

Decent selection of local craft beers, including Kenai River and Midnight Sun beers in cans.

Kenai/Soldotna

Bars/Restaurants

The Back Door Lounge/Sports Bar

47 Spur View Drive Kenai

(907) 283-3241

Smoking. Food served. Good selection of craft beers from local breweries, along with other craft breweries in Alaska.

Buckets Sports Grill

43960 Sterling Highway, Soldotna

(907) 262-7220   **http://www.bucketssportsgrill.com**

Smoke free. Food served. Good beer selection, including a house beer (Buckets Cream Ale) brewed for them by Kassik's Brewery.

Hooligan's Saloon

44715 Sterling Highway, Soldotna

(907) 262-9951   **http://www.hooliganslodge.com/**

Smoking. Food served, including excellent burgers. 18 taps, including local breweries and Rough Draft Series releases from Alaskan Brewing Company. Live entertainment during the summer.

Mykel's Restaurant

5041 Kenai Spur Highway, Soldotna

(907) 262-4305   **http://www.mykels.com/**

Smoke free. Finest dining in town. Full bar with six taps pouring only local beers.

The Pour House Sports Bar

44676 Sterling Highway, Soldotna

(907) 262-GRUB (4782)

Smoke free. Food served. Several local beers on tap, including Kenai River Brewing. Has three "serve yourself" tap tables.

Package/Liquor Stores

Country Liquors

140 South Willow Street, Kenai

(907) 283-7651

Located in the IGA Grocery, this store has the most eclectic selection in the area.

Save-U-More Grocery

35140 Kalifornsky Beach Rd, Soldotna

(907) 262-4245

The liquor store located inside this grocery store has a better than average beer selection.

Festivals

Annual Kenai Peninsula Beer Festival

Held the second Saturday each August in the parking lot of the Sports Center in Soldotna. Organized by the Soldotna Rotary. In 2012, eleven craft breweries from around the state were there. Find it on Facebook for more details.

Images from the 2011 & 2012 Kenai Peninsula Beer Festivals

Homer

Bars/Restaurants

Fat Olives Restaurant

276 Ohlson Lane

(907) 235-8488

Smoke free. Excellent pizzas, calzones, sandwiches, and salads. Homer Brewing Company beers exclusively on tap.

AJ's Oldtown Steakhouse & Tavern

120 W. Bunnell St.

(907) 235-9949

Grass-fed local beef. Frequent live music. Homer Brewing beers on tap.

The Homestead

Mile 8.2 East End Road

(907) 235-8723 **http://homesteadrestaurant.net/**

The finest dining on the Peninsula. Homer Brewing beers on tap.

Land's End Resort

At the very end of the Homer Spit

(907) 235-0400 **http://www.lands-end-resort.com/**

Homer Brewing and other Alaskan beers on tap. Exceptional views.

Café Cups

162 W. Pioneer Ave

907-235-8330 **http://cafecupsofhomer.com/**

Local seafood, pasta, prime ribs, steaks. Homer Brewing beers exclusively on tap, plus bottled beers and wine.

Down East Saloon

3125 East Road

(907) 235-6002 **http://www.downeastsaloon.com/**

Well-kept tap line-up and live music events.

Alice's Champagne Palace

195 E. Pioneer Ave

(907) 235-6909

Located in the heart of the Homer business district. Homer Brewing beers on tap.

Package/Liquor Stores

The Grog Shop

369 East Pioneer Avenue

(907) 235-5101

Best selection of craft beers in town, and likely the Peninsula, including growlers from Homer Brewing Company.

Ring of Fire Meadery

178 East Bunnell Avenue

(907) 235-2656 **http://ringoffiremeadery.com/**

Homer's award-winning meadery. If you enjoy meads, be sure to visit their tasting room.

Bear Creek Winery & Lodging

60203 Bear Creek Drive

(907) 235-8484 **http://www.bearcreekwinery.com/**

Homer is also home to a winery. Their specialty is fruit wines made using local berries.

Kodiak Island

Bars/Restaurants

The Old Powerhouse Restaurant

516 Marine Way East

(907) 481-1088

Smoke free. Full bar with Kodiak Island beers on tap. Exceptional views. Some of the best sushi in Alaska, using amazingly fresh local seafood.

Package/Liquor Stores

Safeway Liquor Store

502 Marine Way

(907) 486-6227

Choices are limited on Kodiak, but this is your best bet.

Alaskan Wilderness Wines

498 Shearwater Way

(907) 539-6684 **http://www.alaskawildwine.com/**

Believe it or not, Kodiak is home to Alaska's oldest winery. Alaskan Wilderness Wines was founded in 1999. In 2011 the company won a gold medal at the Indy International Wine Competition (the largest in the US) for its wild blueberry wine.

Looking Ahead

The craft beer scene on the Kenai Peninsula and Kodiak Island keeps improving. A mere six years ago, Homer Brewing was the only craft brewery in the entire region. Today, there are four breweries and two brewpubs, with rumors of more being planned.

With such tremendous growth in the local beer choices available, the general public on the Peninsula is gradually becoming more and more educated about and interested in craft beers. Local bars and restaurants are slowly becoming more sophisticated in their selection of beers on offer, more informed about the proper serving methods for good beer, and more adept at pairing craft beers with various dishes. The fact that the Kenai Peninsula now supports a very successful annual beer festival is simply another indication that this area is developing a mature craft beer culture, one which is worthy of the difficulty and expense required to travel here to experience it.

I hope you have found the preceding pages informative and helpful. If you are not an Alaskan, I hope they will inspire you to visit our wonderful state and travel to the Kenai Peninsula and Kodiak Island to experience these excellent beers where they are brewed. If you are an Alaskan, I hope you will be encouraged to seek out and experience the unique beers which are produced in our mutual home, especially those from the brewers of the Kenai Peninsula and Kodiak.

But as nice as this region is, there is much more to the state of Alaska and its beers than just what is covered in this book. Look for Volume II of *Beer on the Last Frontier: Anchorage, Fairbanks, and Everything in Between* to be published in 2013, followed by Volume III: *Southeast Alaska Breweries* in 2014.

Until Then, Cheers!